Penmanship

for Christian Writing

Grade 4

Teacher's Manual

Rod and Staff Publishers, Inc.
Crockett, Kentucky 41413
Telephone (606) 522-4348

Acknowledgments

We acknowledge that our omniscient, ever-present Lord has provided us the opportunity and understanding for a venture of this sort. Working closely together, those involved have been enabled by God to establish this new Penmanship series. Our desire has been to please the Lord in providing this course for the Christian school.

We also acknowledge that we have benefited from other handwriting systems in developing the system used in this series. And many teachers were also consulted.

Research and Writing—Daniel Strubhar

Final Editing—Marvin Eicher

Artwork by Lester Miller

Grade Four Curriculum

Pupil's Workbook

Teacher's Manual

Printed in U.S.A.

ISBN 978-07399-0569-2

Catalog no. 15491

12   13   14   15   16   —   20   19   18   17   16   15   14   13   12   11

Table of Contents

Introduction
to Penmanship Series

Penmanship is a subject that many teachers have often overlooked. The reasons are many and varied; but no doubt the main reason is simply that other subjects are considered to be more important, and penmanship has been crowded into the background. But we feel that handwriting needs to hold a prominent place in our Christian school curriculums and that it needs to be taught in an orderly, thorough, and efficient manner. This is the basic reason behind the production of this handwriting series.

The Importance of Teaching Penmanship in Our Schools

1. Good penmanship is a mark of Christian carefulness. God expects His people to be thorough and exact in their activities, not slipshod and careless.

2. Good penmanship is a mark of Christian courtesy. Writing that is difficult to read will not be appreciated by those who must read it.

3. Good penmanship is necessary for good communication. Even though word processors and copiers have taken over in many areas of communication, there are still many purposes for writing that are better accomplished by means of handwriting.

4. Good penmanship is an aid to efficiency. Well-written messages are far less time-consuming to read than those poorly written.

5. Good penmanship will affect students' attitudes. If neat writing is insisted upon, the very act of penning words and sentences in a neat manner will cause students to want to do their best work.

6. Good penmanship on the part of our students will leave a good testimony for our school program. Penmanship is the first thing that impresses the critical eye, before the quality of the work done is apparent.

7. We need to teach good penmanship because it is right. We must do well whatever needs to be done. "Whatsoever thy hand findeth to do, do it with thy might" (Ecclesiastes 9:10).

Our Approach to Handwriting

1. Teaching by Strokes

Teaching handwriting by strokes is the simplest and most efficient way to get the principles of handwriting across. With this approach, the child learns and practices a few basic strokes from which most letters are composed. As he learns these strokes, he has a tool for conquering difficulties in letter formation. In practicing the strokes, he will also become better acquainted with the feel of the basic movements of handwriting, which will help his handwriting to become more efficient and more automatic.

The stroke approach is also beneficial from the teacher's standpoint. It gives him something to teach in handwriting, rather than allowing handwriting instruction to degenerate into nothing more than remedial work. It tends to give a greater enthusiasm for handwriting, because the teacher will know better how to teach it.

Here is how two typical letters are learned by the stroke method:

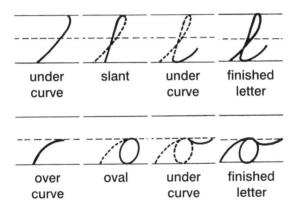

under curve	slant	under curve	finished letter

over curve	oval	under curve	finished letter

2. Teaching Quality

In this course we want to give considerable attention to the teaching of quality. Quality includes slant, alignment, size, proportion, line quality, and spacing, and is a very important part of handwriting (see the following diagrams and definitions). The proper teaching of quality may spell the difference between success and failure in teaching handwriting. The teaching of quality should not be too far removed from the teaching of letter form, so that the children do not separate the two in everyday writing.

Definitions:

    Slant—degree to which a letter is slanted

        consistent slant—all letters slanted the same

        correct slant—straight up and down for first grade manuscript; leaning forward for slant print and cursive

    Alignment—tops and bottoms of letters in straight lines

    Size—largeness or smallness of letters in comparison with what they should be (guidelines for size are specified in each grade)

    Proportion—size of letters or letter parts in relation to other letters or letter parts

    Line quality—degree of lightness or heaviness of writing, related to pencil pressure

    Spacing—distance between words, letters, or sentences

Diagrams of the six areas of quality:

slant and alignment   **size**

too small   too large

proportion   **line quality**   **spacing**

poor   good   good

too dark   too light   poor

3. Difference in Emphasis at Various Grade Levels

In this course we follow an emphasis at each grade level, which builds upon the previous grade, while also reviewing a large part of the previous year's material. The first three grades contain the bulk of new material. For this reason, these grades are the most basic, and the teachers of these grades must be especially careful to give the children a right foundation in handwriting. Grade four contains the least new material. Quality should receive a greater emphasis in grades four to six, and the teachers of these three grades must put forth a continuous effort to keep the students' handwriting up to the standard. In seventh and eighth grades, teachers must emphasize speed, efficiency, and practical handwriting applications in everyday life, while still continuing an emphasis on handwriting quality.

Posture, Pencil Holding, and Paper Placement

Following are standards for proper posture, pencil holding, and paper placement:

1. Posture at seat
   a. Sit back in the seat.
   b. Sit up straight.
   c. Have feet flat on the floor.
   d. Lean slightly forward from the hips.
   e. Have one arm on desk, holding paper, while the other arm writes.

POSTURE

Sit and stand with your back straight and with both feet flat on the floor. Lean forward only a little when you sit at your desk.

2. Posture at blackboard
   a. Stand squarely on both feet directly in front of the blackboard.
   b. Stand back six to twelve inches from the blackboard.

3. Pencil holding
   a. Pencil should be held between the thumb and first finger, resting lightly on the second finger.
   b. Pencil should be held no more firmly than necessary for control.
   c. Pencil must not be cramped or pinched.
4. Chalk holding
   a. Chalk should be held pinched-pencil style, firmly between thumb and first two fingers.
   b. Chalk should point toward the palm of the hand.

PENCIL HOLDING

Hold the pencil so that its top points back over your shoulder. Hold it tightly enough to control it, but do not pinch it.

5. Paper placement
   a. For slant print and cursive writing, right-handers should slant the paper about thirty degrees to the left, and left-handers should slant it toward the right as taught in "Special Instructions for Left-handed Pupils."
   b. The paper should be on the side of the desk toward the arm that will be used to write.

PAPER PLACEMENT

If you write with your right hand, slant the paper to the left. If you write with your left hand, slant the paper to the right far enough so that you can see your writing.

Special Instructions
for Left-handed Pupils

Many teachers seem confused when it comes to teaching left-handed pupils how to write. How should they slant their papers and hold their pencils? How can they write so as to be able to see their writing? How does one prevent them from developing a hooked wrist? This section is intended to answer these questions with sound, positive directions for teachers of left-handers. Although some points may seem strange and even impractical, note carefully that *these principles were developed over several decades* of experimentation with left-handers in many schools. Those left-handers who learned to write by this method developed a neater, more even, and more efficient handwriting style than those taught by other methods. Therefore, unless your left-handed students have already formed poor writing habits, these principles will practically guarantee success if you diligently follow them.

A left-handed pupil must deal with a peculiar handicap when he learns to write. Writing moves from left to right; and for the left-handed person, this means that his writing hand will cover his writing as he moves along. Therefore, many left-handers resort to what seems the simplest solution: a hooked wrist.

However, the hooked wrist is by no means the best solution to this problem. This method makes writing laboriously slow, inefficient, and unpleasant. A far better method is to teach left-handed pupils *from the start* that there are certain things they must do different from right-handed pupils if they are to write well. These differences are listed here.

1. Instead of placing their papers vertically (or slanted to the left for cursive) on their desks, *left-handers must always slant their papers to the right.* In first grade their arms should meet the lines of their papers at right angles; later, *for cursive writing,* their arms should meet their papers *across the lower right-hand corner.* Although this much slant may seem extreme, experience has shown that this is the best way for left-handers to get the proper slant on their letters without using a hooked wrist.

2. *Left-handers should always write toward, not away from, themselves.* If they slant their papers properly, as outlined in number 1 above, they will naturally do this. But when they

write at the blackboard, you will need to make special provisions so that this is possible. *Therefore, give a left-handed child about twice as much room at the blackboard* as what you give to a right-handed child. Then, instead of writing in the space directly in front of him, he can start in the space to his left and write *toward himself* as a left-handed writer should.

3. *Left-handers should hold their pencils exactly the same way that right-handers do.* If they cannot see their writing, either they are holding the pencil too close to the point or their desks are too high. Left-handers can normally write better at a desk lower than usual, because they can better see over their writing hand that way.

4. *If you have a large number of left-handers, group them together* for penmanship classes if possible. This would be especially good in the lower grades, where handwriting habits are first being established. In this way they will not become confused as easily by the right-handers, and you can more quickly see whether they are developing proper habits. Place this group to the right side of the class (as you face the front) so that they can read, as well as write, *toward themselves.*

5. In slant printing and cursive writing, the left-hander's strokes are opposite of the right-hander's. The right-hander *pulls* downstrokes vertically *toward himself,* whereas the left-hander should *push* downstrokes horizontally *away from himself.* Also, the right-hander *pushes* across strokes horizontally *away from himself,* but the left-hander should *pull* across strokes vertically *toward himself.* Study this diagram carefully:

Left-hander	Right-hander

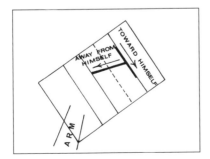 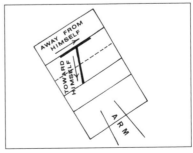

Again, do not be surprised if you have never heard of some of these points. Perhaps *your* teachers never heard of them either! Begin *now* to put them to use. Then you will have the satisfaction of teaching by a definite method that works, and you will have begun on the road to successful handwriting for your left-handed pupils.

Illustrations for proper pencil holding, paper placement, and writing method for left-handed pupils are included in the section "Posture, Pencil Holding, and Paper Placement."

How to Treat the Teacher's Manual

In this course the teacher's manual gives detailed instructions for each lesson: what goals to strive for, how to fill out the workbooks, and how to conduct the class so that the children gain the clearest possible understanding of the lesson. It also gives other diagnostic, remedial, and informative suggestions. And each lesson in the teacher's manual has a reduction of the student workbook lesson for your handy reference.

We suggest that you as a teacher do not overlook the teacher's manual in your preparation for class but that you study it carefully sometime previous to the class period. Especially the inexperienced teacher should read it carefully and thoroughly. Do not let your teaching flounder because of a lack of understanding of the subject material and correct class procedure. Even an experienced teacher does well to study the teacher's manual, although he may already be able to teach the writing of the alphabet successfully. It will help him to understand the approach we are taking in the teaching of this course, and the sequence of thought throughout the lessons.

We suggest not only that you read the manual for each lesson a few hours previous to teaching it but also that you read ahead in the teacher's manual from time to time, to keep abreast of just where you are in accomplishing your goals for the year. You may also find that some of the suggestions that are given in future lessons may be helpful to you in the lessons you are presently teaching, even though they may not always be directly applicable to the present lesson.

Finally, do not be a slave to your teacher's manual. You do not have to accept every suggestion or follow the exact procedure outlined for each class period. The teacher's manual is there to guide the teacher's thinking and is not the final rule of procedure for every situation. However, the basic suggestions were included because they were considered important, and the teacher should consider and use them in one form or another as he plans the lesson.

To the Fourth Grade Teacher

Fourth grade is the beginning of a period in which students tend to hurry through their work and be careless with their writing. Fourth grade is your golden opportunity to arrest this development in its early stages, before it becomes an ingrained habit. Following are some of the basics that should be a part of teaching penmanship to this class.

1. *Maintenance of correct habits of posture, pencil holding, and paper placement.* Reestablish these habits promptly at the beginning, and maintain them throughout the year.

2. *A good teacher example.* You should have good handwriting yourself. It is difficult for a teacher to teach penmanship with any degree of success unless he is able to apply handwriting principles to his own writing. Be willing to teach yourself good handwriting if necessary.

3. *A strong emphasis on review.* You should be aware of how well your pupils are retaining what they have been learning. It would not hurt to take a few minutes in each class to practice a formerly learned letter or stroke, even though the lesson does not mention it.

4. *Teaching each lesson well.* Never be satisfied until you are quite sure that the children are doing the best that they can.

5. *Not allowing significantly poorer writing in daily assignments than in penmanship class.* The pupils must understand that what they learn in penmanship class is to be applied in other subjects as well.

Textbook Goals

The goal in fourth grade is to increase the emphasis on quality while still working hard on proper formation of the letters. In third grade the emphasis was almost exclusively on formation, and in Grades 5 and 6 the emphasis on quality will continue to be strong.

Why We Use Slanted Manuscript

Some teachers may wonder why all the manuscript writing in this book is slanted rather than vertical. There are two basic reasons for this.

1. Slanted printing requires less adjustment for the pupils when they change from manuscript to cursive writing. The position of the paper for slant print as well as for cursive is 30 degrees to the left for right-handed writers. With vertical printing, the children would need

14

to adjust both to slanted writing and to the cursive formations when they make the transition.

2. Slant print can be written faster than vertical print, much as slanted cursive can be written more rapidly than vertical cursive could be. This is because slanted writing follows the natural movements of the hand and arm.

Time Spent in Writing Class

This textbook is designed for one lesson per week for thirty weeks. That is not a full school year, but it is to aid you in having plenty of time to teach each lesson well. The lessons should be evenly spaced with approximately the same amount of time between each lesson. The children should be given one of the practice sentences to write each morning as a warmup exercise on the days that you do not have penmanship class. They can also be permitted to finish some lessons outside the class period if necessary.

Plan to use at least ten minutes if possible to explain each lesson. Take the time necessary to be sure that the children have no unanswered questions before they proceed with the lesson.

Conducting the Class

Follow this basic procedure in teaching the strokes, letters, or areas of quality in each lesson.

1. *Explain and demonstrate the theme of the lesson on the blackboard.*

2. *Have the pupils practice on the blackboard* or on other paper as soon as possible after your demonstration.

3. *Have the pupils work the lesson* under your supervision. Be sure to correct mistakes when you notice them, either on an individual or a class level.

4. *If you are not satisfied with your students' work, keep them practicing* until their writing does come up to that which you consider satisfactory.

What Kind of Work Should You Expect?

You should expect the fourth grader to do fairly accurate work with the cursive small letters, especially after a bit of refresher practice at the beginning of the year. Expect the capitals to be difficult. Be patient, and help your students to master these letters.

Most of your work this year will probably be in the areas of quality. These will no doubt be substandard at first, but do not allow any major deviation in quality then or later. Within a short time the greater deviations should be corrected, and you can spend the rest of the year smoothing out the minor deviations. Strive hard to attain as near perfection as possible.

Left-handed Students

Make it a point to observe at the beginning of the year what is the hand dominance of each child, and respect it. Especially be sure not to neglect the left-handed child. Be satisfied that he is maintaining correct habits; and if he is not, spare no efforts to remedy the situation as soon as possible. (See "Special instructions for Left-handed Pupils.")

Evaluation and Grading

Evaluation involves checking each child's work for errors in form, neatness, and quality. In doing this, you should make notations, telling what is wrong with the writing and how it can be improved.

The evaluation chart grades writing on formation and on seven aspects of quality. Evaluate the pupils' work with reference to the ideal as well as to their previous work (their progress). Count each aspect of writing a certain part of the grade as the numbers on the evaluation chart indicate. As you check, place a red ✕ at each error, and subtract points for that area on the chart. Then when you have finished, add to obtain the total score for the lesson. You will probably need to use some trial and error at first so that the final score is reasonable.

Here are guidelines for grading each area listed on the evaluation chart.

Alignment. Deduct points for letters that do not rest firmly on the baseline or that are too tall in relation to other letters. Drawing lines to show where the writing is out of alignment will show clearly what is wrong. (See the teacher's manual for Lesson 7.)

Slant. Deduct for inconsistent slant as well as for consistent but incorrect slant.

Formation. Penalize for formation if ovals are too flat or too round, if a *t* has a loop, if a slant line is not straight, and so forth. Be reasonable though; it is unrealistic to expect every student's writing to be an exact duplicate of the standard.

16

Word Spacing. Spaces between words should be about as wide as the cursive small letter *a*. Deduct for spacing that is too narrow or too wide, or if it is inconsistent.

Letter Spacing. This refers to spacing between letters within words. Deduct for letters that are crowded too close together or spread too far apart.

Neatness. This area is closely related to some of the others, but it is a more general category. Unclosed ovals and improperly dotted *i*'s should be penalized in the neatness category, as well as smudges and wrinkles (carelessness in general).

Size. The size of writing refers to how large or how small it is in general, as well as to the size of individual words or phrases in relation to others. Just a few *letters* of the wrong size would be penalized in the category of alignment.

Proportion. This refers to the size of letter parts in relation to each other. Deduct points, for example, if the upper half of capital *B* is conspicuously larger or smaller than the lower half.

Miscellaneous Helps

1. As an aid to your children when they practice on the blackboard, you should draw lines for them to write on. The simplest way is to use a music scorer. For fourth grade size writing, leave all the pieces of chalk in.

2. Remember the extra practice paper on the back of each page. Do not hesitate to use it if you feel that your students need extra practice on paper.

3. Help the children to make the adjustment from writing on paper with alignment lines to writing on paper with only a base line, as they must do in other subjects. Explain that they will need to do careful estimation when there are no alignment lines to indicate the correct heights. The pupils should try to maintain the same proportion as when there are alignment lines.

Lesson 1

Introduction

Aim of the Lesson

To help the children recall penmanship skills that may be rusty after a summer's disuse; to get them started writing smaller, normal-size letters.

Comments to the Teacher

1. In this lesson you will need to lay a good foundation for penmanship for the year. Here are some things to pay special attention to:
   a. Proper posture, paper placement, and pencil holding. Be sure all is correct right from the beginning. Guidelines for these areas are found in the teacher's introduction and in the front of the pupil's books.
   b. Do all within your power to achieve a high penmanship standard for the children on every paper, not just in penmanship lessons. It can be done if you insist upon it. One possible way would be to take papers from any subject to obtain some penmanship grades or to display for the other children to judge the penmanship.
   c. Start the children out right in quality and formation. Begin watching immediately for areas that need correction.
2. Use the evaluation chart to grade only the last row of each lesson unless it is obvious that you should do otherwise. This makes scoring much simpler. (Note that the last row has no alignment lines; this is to have the students put to practice what they have learned, as they must do on regular paper.)
3. In conducting the class, discuss the paragraphs at the top of the page, and give a general introduction. Explain that this year different animals are mentioned in different lessons, and that the children will be writing sentences about them. After you have mentioned the points you think are important, have the children proceed with the lesson under your supervision.
4. Lines 5 and 6 on the pupil's page include letters from the simple as well as the more difficult categories of the cursive letters. Your

Lesson 1   Introduction

The Bible tells us, "God made the beast of the earth after his kind, . . . and every thing that creepeth upon the earth after his kind: and God saw that it was good" (Genesis 1:25).

God liked animals, and we do too. From the enormous elephant to the smallest mouse, animals are interesting to observe and learn about, because God made them well.

Can you make letters and words well too, so that they are pleasant to look at and read? Try to do that this year, in this penmanship book as well as in all your work.

Copy these sentences on the lines below them.

How happy we are that God has created the animal world!

How pleasant it is to have dogs, cats, cows, sheep, and horses

in our world!

Copy each letter at least twice in the spaces following.

s

r

G

e

l

m

Write this sentence below: **We can write well if we try hard.**

Alignment	15	Letter Spacing	10
Slant	15	Neatness	20
Formation	15	Size	10
Word Spacing	5	Proportion	10
		Total	___

3

students' success with them will tell you much about their present handwriting ability.

Practice Sentences

1. God sees even the sparrow fall.
2. God made many animals on the sixth day.
3. All of God's creation is good.
4. The animals in this book are called mammals.

Lesson 2   **Slant Print Review** *(Part 1)*

The lion is often called the king of the beasts because he is powerful and majestic. He has a kingly roar too! Lions live in Africa and Asia, where they hunt and kill other animals for food. Although lions are fierce animals, they also like to spend much of their time lying in shady spots resting or sleeping.

Do you remember how to make the strokes of slant print? They are the oval ($\circ$); the curve ($\sim$); the slant (/); the across line (—); the backward slanting line (\ ); and the forward slanting line (/).

$A\ B\ C\ D\ E\ F\ G\ H\ I\ J\ K\ L\ M\ N\ O\ P\ Q\ R\ S\ T\ U\ V\ W\ X\ Y\ Z$

$a\ b\ c\ d\ e\ f\ g\ h\ i\ j\ k\ l\ m\ n\ o\ p\ q\ r\ s\ t\ u\ v\ w\ x\ y\ z$

On the lines below, copy each letter of the alphabet three times in slant print.

Neatness   40
Formation   40
Slant   20
       Total ____

Lesson 2

Slant Print Review *(Part 1)*

Aim of the Lesson

To review the proper way of making the letters in slant print and of writing them smoothly and neatly.

Comments to the Teacher

1. Begin with drill on the strokes used in slant print. Have the children make each stroke in the air, on the blackboard, or on paper. (These strokes are illustrated in the upper right corner of the pupil's lesson.)

2. Remind the children of some basic principles of slant print.

   a. Since the writing is slanted, the papers should be slanted.

   b. There are no circles in slant print, only ovals.

   c. Capital and tall letters are twice as tall as small letters.

3. After you have reviewed these basics, have the children go ahead with the lesson.

4. The children might lack enthusiasm for printing and be inclined to do a poor job at this age. Remind them that when they grow up, they will often need to print. Give some examples, such as filling in forms or making signs.

Practice Sentences

1. Only a male lion has a mane.
2. A family of lions is called a pride.
3. Christ is called the Lion of Judah.
4. The righteous are bold as a lion.

Lesson 3   Slant Print Review *(Part 2)*

The raccoon has a "mask" of black hair across its face, and rings around its tail. It likes to wade in streams and ponds, hunting for crayfish, frogs, and fish. Many raccoons have a habit of dunking their food in water before eating it. Young raccoons are sometimes kept for pets because they are intelligent animals.

There is more to good slant print than making the letters correctly. You need to space the letters and words the right distance apart too. You also need to make them the right height, and you need to make them neatly.

Copy this verse and its reference on the lines below.

"And God said, Let the earth bring forth the living creature after his kind, cattle and creeping thing, and beast of the earth after his kind: and it was so." Genesis 1:24

Copy each letter twice.

2   2

P   P

Formation	40	Neatness	20
Slant	10	Height and	10
Word Spacing	10	Proportion	
Letter Spacing	10	Total	

Lesson 3

Slant Print Review *(Part 2)*

Aim of the Lesson

To help the children write words and sentences in slant print neatly with proper spacing.

Comments to the Teacher

1. For drill, have the children make letter *l*'s in slant print on the blackboard one after the other, trying to space them evenly. Then have them make "words": three *l*'s, space, three *l*'s, space, and so forth.

2. Discuss height and spacing of slant print. Explain just how far apart words should be spaced (the width of the letter *a*). Also demonstrate proper distance between letters within a word, to refresh the children's minds. The letters should not overlap (*to*); rather, there should be a narrow space between the widest parts of each letter (*tb*).

3. Often with slant print it is difficult for the children to maintain consistent spacing and formation. Work on even alignment, consistent slant, and regular spacing and form.

4. Evaluate the entire lesson this time.

Practice Sentences

1. The raccoon eats crayfish, frogs, and fish.
2. An adult raccoon weighs about 15 pounds (7 kg).
3. The crab-eating raccoon lives in South America.
4. Raccoons can make good pets.

Note: The measurements in this course are given in both U.S. and metric units. For the practice sentences, you will probably want to have your students write only the units with which they are most familiar.

25

Lesson 4 Numerals Review

Chipmunks live in underground burrows, but they often come out and dash about in search of food. They eat things like nuts, seeds, and dried fruits. Often they will sit on their hind feet, holding the food between their forepaws. If chipmunks are fed regularly, they may become quite tame.

You use numerals every day in arithmetic. Do you make them clearly and neatly so that you can do accurate work?

Practice these numerals in the spaces following them.

1

2

3

4

5

6

7

8

9

0

Copy each problem several times.

4 + 6 = 10

15 - 2 = 13

8 × 9 = 72

Neatness	20	Formation	20
Slant	20	Spacing	20
Size	20	Total	

Lesson 4

Numerals Review

Aim of the Lesson

To teach the children to write numerals neatly.

Comments to the Teacher

1. The main goal in practicing numerals at this level is to get the children to make neat, legible numbers for mathematics classes.

2. You know how easy it is for some pupils' mathematics papers to degenerate into "chicken tracks." So put forth a real effort to keep your children's numerals legible. Insist that they write their numerals neatly on every arithmetic paper. Have them recopy substandard work. Also instruct them as to how you want their problems written—either one row or two rows of numerals per line ($\frac{5}{2\sqrt{10}}$ or $2\sqrt{10}$)—and work for consistency with every paper. At this level you will probably want only one row per line.

3. The numerals are written the approximate size that the children will use in arithmetic. At this stage there is little point in making them very large—the children never write them that way.

4. Call attention to the proper formation of each numeral, but most of all insist on good quality. The numerals taught in lower-grade levels of this series are the manuscript style. In this lesson, the cursive style is introduced, which will continue to be the style taught in this course.

5. Be sure that the mathematical symbols (+, −, ×, =) are made legibly and correctly.

6. Evaluate on the basis of the full page this time.

Practice Sentences

1. A chipmunk hibernates in winter.
2. Chipmunks carry food in pouches in their cheeks.
3. Chipmunks like nuts and seeds.
4. A chipmunk is a wonder of God's creation.

Lesson 5   Stroke Review *(Part 1)*

The pronghorn is a deerlike animal of deserts and open prairies. It is known for its rapid speed in running, which is up to 50 miles per hour (80 km/h) for short distances. Pronghorns live almost all over the western United States.

What are letters made of? They are composed of individual strokes. Each person does not just make them as he thinks they should look. Instead, we follow a plan for each letter, and each plan is simply a group of strokes.

Fill each line with copies of the forms below.

Alignment	15	Letter Spacing	10
Slant	15	Neatness	20
Formation	15	Size	10
Word Spacing	5	Proportion	5
		Total	___

*Write this sentence in cursive: **Pronghorns can run very fast.***

11

Lesson 5

Stroke Review *(Part 1)*

Aim of the Lesson

To review the basic strokes of cursive writing and to give practice in forming them.

Comments to the Teacher

1. Discuss the paragraph on strokes in the upper right corner of the lesson.

2. Explain the multiple ovals and "ups and downs." Have the children practice making them on the blackboard.

3. Discuss the four strokes mentioned in the lesson (oval, slant, undercurve, and overcurve). These are the basic strokes that make up small cursive letters. This lesson does not include the retrace, which is basically a short slant line, or the loop, which is used only in capital letters.

4. Try to get the children to make the lines of the multiple ovals and "ups and downs" as evenly as possible. They should make six ovals or peaks in each set.

5. Work on smoothness and evenness of formation with the four basic strokes. Do not let the children make them so slowly that they "draw" them. They should make the strokes quickly enough to get the feel of them.

6. The last sentence of this lesson and following lessons is to be written in cursive. It is the sentence upon which your evaluation is to be based, with special emphasis on the area drilled in each lesson.

Practice Sentences

1. The pronghorn is not a true antelope.
2. The pronghorn's color is brown and creamy white.
3. A frightened pronghorn raises a white "flag" of hair.
4. Pronghorns eat low plants like sagebrush.

Lesson 6   Stroke Review *(Part 2)*

The Canada otter is an animal that lives in many parts of North America. It is long and slender like a weasel. The otter feels the most at home in water. Otters are playful animals. They enjoy sliding down steep muddy banks on their stomach.

Today we will practice forms that are combined strokes. Double curves are made of two curves in opposite directions. Loops are also made of opposite curves, but they are put together differently from double curves. Round tops and sharp tops are made of curves and slant lines. These two combinations are used very often in handwriting.

Fill the space after each combination or letter with copies of it.

Write on the line below: ***The otter is much like a weasel.***

Alignment	15	Letter Spacing	10
Slant	15	Neatness	20
Formation	15	Size	10
Word Spacing	5	Proportion	10
		Total	

Lesson 6

Stroke Review *(Part 2)*

Aim of the Lesson

To review four combinations of strokes that are used frequently in cursive writing.

Comments to the Teacher

1. Discuss the paragraph in the upper right corner. Then have the children make these strokes in the air before doing the lesson.
2. As the children do the lesson, be sure that
   a. the curves in their double curves are well balanced without any sharp points at any place. They should be graceful and even.
   b. the loop is properly proportioned and well shaped. The enclosed part should be oval, not rounded.
   c. the round top has a rounded curve; it does not look like this: Λ. The slant line should be straight.
   d. the sharp top has a straight back and a rounded curve. The undercurve should not be so deeply curved that it follows the slant most of the way like this: $\mathcal{J}$.
3. Strive for even gracefulness in the making of each combination so that every student's writing becomes consistently clear and readable.

Practice Sentences

1. Otters often play on mud slides.
2. An otter's diet is fish, frogs, and other small animals.
3. The weight of an adult otter is 20 pounds (9 kg).
4. The sea otter lives along the ocean.

Lesson 7   Quality

One animal God made can probably chop down trees better than you can. How does it do this—with an ax or a chain saw? No, it uses its teeth. The beaver's strong, sharp teeth are especially made for the job of felling trees.

Beavers mainly eat bark, twigs, roots, and water plants.

The beaver does a good job of building a beaver house, and you should do a good job of building letters and words. That is, your writing should have good quality. This includes such things as giving all the letters the same slant, making letters the right height, keeping tops and bottoms of letters in a straight line, and keeping words and letters properly spaced.

Copy the word or words in the spaces following.

slant, size

alignment

height

spacing

proportion

neatness

Write this sentence: ***Beavers build their houses well.***

Alignment	15	Letter Spacing	10
Slant	15	Neatness	20
Formation	15	Size	10
Word Spacing	5	Proportion	10
		Total	

Lesson 7

Quality

Aim of the Lesson

To help the children make letters of good quality, learning again the different aspects that are involved in good quality.

Comments to the Teacher

1. Demonstrate what is meant by each area of quality. Show letters of good quality, and then contrast them with letters of poor quality in each area. If you need a better understanding of the areas of quality, turn back to the section on quality in the teacher's introduction to the book.

2. Have the children practice writing words, emphasizing different areas of quality each time.

3. As they go ahead with the lesson, they should work especially on the area of quality that they are writing about. Then when they write the last sentence, they should try to put all the areas of quality to practice. Teach them to look at their writing critically to see how nearly perfect it is in each area.

4. Evaluate the different areas of quality by drawing lines to show how each child's work compares with the ideal. Examples: *alignment; slant.*

Practice Sentences

1. Beavers make houses of tree limbs.
2. Long ago beaver pelts were in great demand.
3. The beaver has a wide, flat tail.
4. The beaver uses its tail to steer when it swims.

Lesson 8   Slant

What is the tallest animal living? The giraffe, of course! God has given him long legs and a long neck that make him as much as 16 feet (5 meters) tall. Because he is so tall, he can reach the leaves high on trees for his food.

The slant of the giraffe's neck should show us something about our writing. It is very nearly like the slant that our letters should have. Try to keep your letters slanted the same as the giraffe's neck—all the time.

Copy these words on the line below them. Use proper slant.

proper slant   improper slant   Which is for me?

Write your full name twice with proper slant.

Copy this sentence with proper slant.

God gave the giraffe long legs and a long neck.

Write each letter twice with proper slant.

t   d   l   e   a   p

*Write below: **My letters should slant like his neck.***

Alignment	15	Letter Spacing 10
Slant	15	Neatness 20
Formation	15	Size 10
Word Spacing	5	Proportion 10
		Total ___

17

Lesson 8

Slant

Aim of the Lesson

To teach the children to apply the principles that contribute to good slant in writing.

Comments to the Teacher

1. Slant is one of the most important aspects of good handwriting. Do not spare in teaching it well. Have the children practice and practice until they can maintain correct slant with every letter.

2. There are two keys to good slant in writing: a properly slanted paper, and an even style of writing in which the hand moves smoothly across the page. "Windshield wiper" handwriting, a style in which the hand is continually rotated about the wrist, will not produce consistent slant. Work on having the children develop the habit of using these two keys.

3. The children should also have good slant in their work in other subjects.

4. Remember to be more exacting in your evaluation of slant in the last line than you are of the other areas of quality.

Practice Sentences

1. A giraffe can run 30 miles per hour (50 km/h).
2. Giraffes can go for weeks without water.
3. Usually a giraffe makes no noise.
4. The giraffe is colored brown and white.

Lesson 9   Letters With Ovals

The armadillo is one of the "hardest" animals that God has made. It can roll up in a tight ball when danger threatens, and then few animals can get a grip on the hard, bony plates in its hide. The name *armadillo* is Spanish for "little armored thing."

It is very important that you learn to make the oval correctly if you hope to become a good writer. Not many letters have a complete oval, but three of the ones that do are used often. So learn to make well the letters with ovals.

Fill the first line with small ovals.

o

Practice each letter in the space following it.

c o a

c o a a

c o g g

c o g g

Copy each word once.

armadillo   go   quickly

Write this sentence: **We want to do what is right.**

Alignment	15	Letter Spacing	20
Slant	15	Neatness	15
Formation	15	Size	10
Word Spacing	5	Proportion	10
		Total	___

Lesson 9

Letters With Ovals

Aim of the Lesson

To aid the children in forming smoothly and accurately the letters *o, a, g,* and *q.*

Comments to the Teacher

1. It would be good to begin this class with an air drill on the oval, and then drill on paper. Remind the pupils of proper oval formation—not too round, not too flat, but made with a normal overcurve-undercurve movement of the hand.

2. As the children work, also be sure that they maintain correct *slant.* Good learning adds one principle to another; it does not drop one to learn another. Demonstrate the proper slant for these letters.

3. With oval letters, you need to watch that the ovals are always *closed.* Be firm about unclosed letters; it is usually laziness that leaves them open. Deduct points in the "neatness" category of evaluation when letters are not closed.

4. With the letter *g,* be sure the final overcurve crosses on the base line. It is to be a smooth overcurve, not a double curve (*g*).

5. With the letter *o,* be sure the final undercurve is not so deep that the letter looks like an *a;* nor should it be so shallow that it looks like a straight-across line.

Practice Sentences

1. An armadillo can dig itself rapidly into the ground.
2. The giant armadillo lives in South America.
3. One food armadillos like is ants.
4. Some small armadillos are only 5 inches (13 cm) long.

Lesson 10   Letters With Upper Loops

Bats fly at night and sleep during the day. They eat insects which they catch while flying. Bats are not birds. They are mouselike animals covered with fur. Their wings are covered with thin skin. Bats can fly without bumping into anything when it is completely dark.

Loops are made with an undercurve and a slant, and they should be formed smoothly and evenly. Remember:
1. The undercurve needs a hook at the top.
2. The slant line must be straight.
3. The slant line must cross the curve at the right place.

Copy these letters to the end of each line.

l l l l

l l f f

l l h h h

l l l l l

l l l

Copy this sentence twice.

Bats look ugly.

*Write this sentence: **Most bats eat harmful insects.***

Alignment	15	Letter Spacing	10
Slant	15	Neatness	20
Formation	15	Size	10
Word Spacing	5	Proportion	10
		Total___	

Lesson 10

Letters With Upper Loops

Aim of the Lesson

To teach the children to form the letters *b, f, h, k,* and *l* accurately and smoothly.

Comments to the Teacher

1. Have the children practice the upper-loop formation over and over on the blackboard to refresh the basic feel of the combination.

2. Discuss the material in the upper right corner of the lesson with the pupils.

3. Remind the children of proportional relationships in these letters. The slant crosses the undercurve at one-third full height; and the last parts of *b, h,* and *k* are one-third height as well.

4. Remind the children also that loops should not be too big and wide, nor should they be too narrow.

5. Slant is critical with upper-loop letters. Be sure the children are slanting properly.

6. Smooth formation of these letters is the thing to work for. If any letters can be formed gracefully, its should be these.

Practice Sentences

1. Bats are very useful because they eat insects.
2. A vampire bat stays alive by sucking blood.
3. A flying fox bat has a wingspread of over 4 feet (1 meter).
4. The bat uses high-pitched squeaks to keep from hitting things.

Lesson 11   Letters With Lower Loops

What animal has very long ears, long hind legs, and lives on the prairies of the western United States? A jack rabbit, of course! The jack rabbit is actually a hare, not a rabbit. Hares have longer legs and ears than rabbits, and they do not dig burrows like rabbits do.

When you make lower loops, remember:
1. The slant line must be straight.
2. The loop should extend below the base line as far as the *t* rises above the base line.
3. The overcurve should cross the slant line exactly at the base line.

Practice each letter in the space following it.

ᴵ ᵒ ᵍ ᵍ

ᴵ ᶠ ᶠ ᶠ

ᴵ ᴬ ᴺ ʸ ʸ

ᴵ ᵒ ᵍ ᵍ

Copy this sentence in the line below it.

Long ago, jack rabbits provided meat for farmers.

Write this sentence: **It is a jack rabbit, of course!**

Alignment	15	Letter Spacing	10
Slant	15	Neatness	20
Formation	15	Size	10
Word Spacing	5	Proportion	10
		Total	___

23

Lesson 11

Letters With Lower Loops

Aim of the Lesson

To teach the children to form the letters *g, j, y,* and *z* accurately and neatly.

Comments to the Teacher

1. Some of the letters fall into more than one category, and the letter *g* is one of them. Although this letter has already been practiced, it is again studied here because it should also be seen as a lower-loop letter.

2. Have the children air drill on the slant-overcurve combination with you.

3. Demonstrate the material in the upper right corner of the lesson for the children.

4. Show correct and incorrect formation. Associate slant with the lower-loop letters as you did for the upper-loop letters. Insist upon correct slant.

5. Watch that the lower loops are of consistent length and shape. The shape should be much like that of the upper loops—not too wide; neither should the loop be nearly closed. Continue to make sure that the final stroke is not a double curve.

6. The letter *z* sometimes presents complications. Its lower loop is not a slant and an overcurve, but rather an undercurve and an overcurve. Help the children make this letter with a proper shape and slant. Remember that the strokes of the letter are *overcurve, slant, small hook, undercurve,* and *overcurve.*

7. Evaluate both of the last sentences in this lesson. They drill lower loops as well as upper loops.

Practice Sentences

1. A jack rabbit can run 30 miles per hour (50 km/h).
2. The jack rabbit lives in dry areas.
3. Farmers today do not like the jack rabbit.
4. The jack rabbit eats the farmers' crops.

41

Lesson 12   Alignment

The largest animal in the world is the whale. One whale grew to be over 100 feet (30 meters) long, and it weighed over 280,000 pounds (130,000 kg). Some whales could easily swallow a man.

We all like things to be straight. We like straight rooms, straight rows in our gardens, and straight, smooth highways. God likes things straight and in order too.

Alignment in handwriting means to keep the tops and bottoms of letters even and straight where they should be. How well can you do?

Write these words correctly in the line below.

good alignment   poor alignment

Copy this verse.

"God is not the author of confusion, but of peace, as in all

churches of the saints." I Corinthians 14:33

Write this sentence: ***Is my alignment like the whale's back?***

Alignment	15	Letter Spacing	10
Slant	15	Neatness	20
Formation	15	Size	10
Word Spacing	5	Proportion	10
		Total	___

Lesson 12

Alignment

Aim of the Lesson

To teach the children the importance and the practice of even alignment in handwriting.

Comments to the Teacher

1. Begin by discussing the material in the upper right corner of the lesson.

2. Using the word *animal,* have the children practice on the blackboard, striving to keep all the small letters even in height and even along the bottom.

3. Before the children begin the lesson, stress *how* they can keep their letters even at the top and firmly resting on the base line. It simply means to be careful that every stroke goes neither higher nor lower than it should.

4. Demonstrate good alignment on the blackboard.

5. As the children proceed with the lesson, emphasize alignment by holding a ruler across the tops of their letters when they are out of line. Also call the child's attention to it when his letters are not resting firmly on the base line.

6. A "windshield wiper" type of writing promotes poor alignment. Be sure your children are moving their wrists smoothly across the page. Some children will say they can't, but you should insist that they *can,* with practice.

7. Be exacting with alignment in your evaluation of this lesson. Draw lines to show where the children's writing is out of alignment.

Example: *like*

Practice Sentences

1. Whales are hunted for their oil.
2. Whales breathe air as we do.
3. Whales are found only in oceans.
4. A whale is not a fish but a mammal.

Lesson 13   Letters With Upper Stems

You have probably never seen a wild yak. The yak is a wild ox that feeds on tough grasses in central Asia, in the country of Tibet. The yak is a big animal and may grow to over six feet high at the shoulder.

Most letters are either tall or short. But three letters are different. The letters *d*, *p*, and *t* are of medium height. They are twice as tall as short letters, but not so tall as the tallest letters.

Practice each letter in the space following.

ᴄ ᴅ ᴅ ᴅ

ɭ ɭ ƥ ƥ

ɭ ɭ ƭ

Copy each word five times in two columns.

paddle   tapped   petted

Write this sentence: ***He carried a package on a yak.***

Alignment	15	Letter Spacing	10
Slant	15	Neatness	20
Formation	15	Size	10
Word Spacing	5	Proportion	10
		Total	

27

Lesson 13

Letters With Upper Stems

Aim of the Lesson

To teach the proper formation of the letters *d, p,* and *t.*

Comments to the Teacher

1. Alignment and proportion come clearly into focus with these three letters. Many people's writing is vague as to just how high *d, t,* and *p* should go, and there is often a great variation in the heights. It is up to you as a teacher to teach these letters so that *your* students know how to make them.

2. Begin class by going over the material in the upper right corner of the page.

3. Demonstrate clearly on the blackboard the difference in height between these three letters and the tall and short letters of the alphabet. The children will need to put this difference into practice in lines 4, 5, and 6.

4. Be sure the children make the slant lines of these letters straight.

5. Be sure that all *d*'s and *p*'s are closed, and that there are no loops in any of the stems.

Practice Sentences

1. The yak can enjoy below-zero temperatures.
2. Some yaks have horns as long as 40 inches (1 meter).
3. People of Asia use the yak to bear burdens.
4. The yak is a very strong animal.

Lesson 14   Short Letters Beginning With Undercurves

What animal has ears 5 feet (1.5 meters) long and lives from 60 to 80 years? It is also the biggest land animal. It is the elephant. Elephants have a trunk and two sharp tusks. They can be trained to do many useful jobs.

Eighteen letters of our alphabet are short letters; they do not rise as high as the *t*, *d*, or *p*. Today we will practice those that begin with undercurves.

Most of the letters of this lesson we use at least once in almost every sentence that we write. How well can you make them?

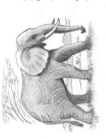

Copy each letter in the spaces following.

ı ı ı ı

ı ı ı

ı ı ı ı

ı ı ı

ı ı ı ı ı ı ı

*Write this sentence: **Let's use our small ears to listen.***

Alignment	15	Letter Spacing	10
Slant	15	Neatness	20
Formation	15	Size	10
Word Spacing	5	Proportion	10
		Total ___

Lesson 14

Short Letters Beginning With Undercurves

Aim of the Lesson

To help the children learn to form well these six important letters: *i, e, r, s, u,* and *w.*

Comments to the Teacher

1. Have the children air drill the undercurve briefly.
2. Discuss the material in the upper right corner of the lesson.
3. Be careful to explain and demonstrate carefully the formations and relationships between these letters. Some to take note of are as follows:
   a. The letters *e* and *i* are related. The letter *e* simply has a hook and loop and is minus a dot. Try to insure that these letters maintain straight backs. The loop in *e* should not be too wide or too narrow.
   b. The letters *r* and *s* are related in that the points of both rise slightly above the first alignment line. Be sure the children pay careful attention to the stroke formation of *r* (undercurve, undercurve, slant, undercurve).
   c. The letter *u* is basically a double *i* without dots. The letter *w* is like a triple *i* except that the last slant is only a retrace. Be sure spacing between each point in these two letters is consistent.
4. The letters in Lessons 14 and 15 are called short letters because they do not have upper or lower loops, nor do they have upper stems. The two short letters with ovals (*a* and *o*) were drilled in Lesson 9.

Practice Sentences

1. An elephant uses its trunk as a hand and an arm.
2. An elephant can be dangerous when it is angry.
3. A large elephant can drink 50 gallons (200 liters) of water a day.
4. Elephants live both in Africa and in Asia.

Lesson 15 Short Letters Beginning With Overcurves

Chimpanzees are large animals of the monkey family. They grow to be 3 to 5 feet (1 to 1.6 meters) tall, and they weigh about 100 to 175 pounds (45 to 80 kg) when fully grown. Chimpanzees are covered with long, black hair.

Today we will be practicing the short letters that begin with overcurves. These letters are important, although they are not written so often as the letters that begin with undercurves.

Can you make a good overcurve stroke? A correctly made overcurve is smooth, and it does not curve either too much or too little.

Practice each letter in the spaces following.

ℓ ℓ ℓ

ι ι m m m m

ι ι r m m

ι ι n n n

ι ι n n

ι

ε

n

r

w

*Write this sentence: **Is a chimpanzee a very good pet?***

Alignment	15	Letter Spacing	10
Slant	15	Neatness	20
Formation	15	Size	10
Word Spacing	5	Proportion	10
		Total ___	

31

Lesson 15

Short Letters Beginning With Overcurves

Aim of the Lesson

To help the children learn to make the letters *c, m, n, v,* and *x* neatly and accurately.

Comments to the Teacher

1. Go over the material in the upper right corner of the page.
2. Immediately following, have the children air drill on the overcurve stroke, and then drill on paper as well.
3. Concentrate on a good formation of the overcurve, especially emphasizing the last paragraph of the lesson introduction.
4. Be sure the letter c has good form. It should not be one big rounded curve like this: *℃*; rather, there should be almost a point between the second and third strokes, like this: *ㄴ*.
5. With *m* and *n*, be sure there is consistency in the distance between each "leg" of the letter. Within each letter, space should be consistent, and every letter should look the same.
6. With *m, n, v,* and *x,* be sure that the overcurve-slant combinations are made well.

Practice Sentences

1. Chimpanzees can do many things that people can do.
2. Chimpanzees can be taught to ride bicycles.
3. Africa is the home of the chimpanzee.
4. A chimpanzee's main food is wild fruit.

Lesson 16   Size and Proportion

The size of your writing is important. Why? Well, if it is too small, your writing is hard to read. If it is too large, the lines of writing run into each other and it is still hard to read.

Have you ever seen a letter just tall enough that you could not tell whether it was an *l* or an *e*? If you have, the problem was that the letter did not have good proportion.

Write these words correctly on the line below them.

too large   too small   incorrect proportion

Copy in the lines below.

Tall giraffes, medium horses, short gophers—God's animals

are always the right size and proportion.

*Write this sentence: **Does my writing have good proportion?***

Alignment	15	Letter Spacing	10
Slant	15	Neatness	20
Formation	15	Size	10
Word Spacing	5	Proportion	10
		Total	___

33

Lesson 16

Size and Proportion

Aim of the Lesson

To teach the children carefulness in keeping their writing the proper size and proportion.

Comments to the Teacher

1. Go over the material at the top of the lesson with the children.

2. Go over the words in line 1. Discuss the incorrectness of each set of words.

3. Much of the secret of good proportion is simply remembering how high each part of each letter goes and always making it exactly that height.

4. The children need to have a basic understanding of the three sizes of letters (short, medium, and tall). They should have acquired this by now in their study of the letters, but be sure they understand the proportional relationship as well.

5. Tell your pupils that they will probably have the most problems with size and proportion on papers where there are no lines to guide the size. They should use the writing size in the book as a guide for the rest of their writing. To test their ability to put to practice the principles of proportion, you may want the children to write the lesson on regular paper also, and compare it with their work in the book.

Practice Sentences

1. Jesus is the only way of salvation.
2. None can come to God except by Him.
3. More should learn to love Jesus.
4. Christ wants all men to be saved.

Lesson 17   Capitals With
Beginning Loops (*Part 1*)

Jesus once called Herod a fox because Herod was sly and cunning. Foxes are very smart animals. They use many tricks to keep man and his dogs from catching them.

We do not use nearly as many capital letters as we do small letters. But maybe we use more of them than we think. All names and sentences must begin with capital letters. This means that almost any word could begin with a capital letter sometime.

Copy each letter in the spaces following.

    T

   T T T

   N N N

   H H H

   M M M

   M M

   Q

Alignment	15	Letter Spacing	10
Slant	15	Neatness	20
Formation	15	Size	10
Word Spacing	5	Proportion	10
		Total	___

*Write these names: **Tom, Faye, Hilda, Karen, Mary, Nevin, Quincy***

Lesson 17

Capitals With
Beginning Loops *(Part 1)*

Aim of the Lesson

To teach the children to make the capital letters *T, F, H, K, M, N,* and *Q* smoothly and accurately.

Comments to the Teacher

1. After discussing the paragraphs at the top of the page, explain and demonstrate the proper formation of the loop to refresh the children's minds. The loop is one of the harder writing forms to make smoothly and accurately.

2. Be sure the children's loops are closed.
Be sure they are not too long or too short.
Be sure the second curve is gently curved, not straight or sharply curved.

3. The capital letters *T* and *F* are always complex and difficult to make smoothly. The secret to good formation is learning to make double curves smoothly, with the two curves well balanced. Be sure the children discern the difference between cursive capital *T* and *F*.

4. Note similarities between the letters *H* and *K*. The letter *K* has several double curves.

5. The letter *M* and *N* should have descending humps. Spacing between the "legs" of these letters should be consistent.

6. Note that the double curve of the letter *Q* drops gracefully below the base line.

Practice Sentences

1. The Arctic fox changes from brown to white in winter.
2. The gray fox is able to climb trees.
3. The kit fox is a very small prairie fox.
4. The red fox is hunted for its fur.

Lesson 18   Capitals With
                 Beginning Loops *(Part 2)*

What would you call an animal that looks like a horse, has black and white stripes, and lives in Africa? It is a zebra. The zebra lives on the grassy plains just on the edge of a desert.

The letters in today's lesson begin in the same way as did the letters in Lesson 17. They all begin with loops. Did you make the beginning loops in that lesson smoothly and correctly? Today, with your teacher's help, try to do even better.

Practice each letter in the spaces following.

Write these names: **Upton, Virgil, Wanda, Yvonne, Zelda**

Alignment	15	Letter Spacing	10
Slant	15	Neatness	20
Formation	15	Size	10
Word Spacing	5	Proportion	10
		Total	___

Lesson 18

Capitals With
Beginning Loops *(Part 2)*

Aim of the Lesson

To teach the children to make the capital letters *U, V, W, X, Y,* and *Z* smoothly and accurately.

Comments to the Teacher

1. Read and discuss in class the paragraph in the upper right corner of the page.

2. Again concentrate on proper formation of the loop, emphasizing the same points as in the last lesson.

3. The letters *U, V,* and *W* are formed in regular ways, so check the letters primarily for accuracy. Be sure the children form the letter *W* this way: *𝒴*, not like this: *𝒲*.

4. Be sure the two parts of the letter *X* touch in the middle. Curves should be gentle, with something of a point between the last two curves.

5. With the letter *Y,* the second peak should be lower than the first. In other words, a line drawn across the top should descend from left to right.

6. The "back" of the letter *Z,* though made with curves, should look straight.

Practice Sentences

1. A zebra's worst enemy is the lion.
2. The zebra often has a bad temper.
3. A zebra is not tame like a horse.
4. Zebras usually travel in groups.

Lesson 19   Proper Margins

There is an animal that you are wise to keep away from. No, it does not bite or sting—it simply smells! God has given the skunk this unusual way of protecting itself.

One thing that the skunk teaches us is to stay a safe distance away. You should also stay a proper distance away from the edge of your paper. Your paper will look much neater, and your writing will be easier to read too.

Write Proverbs 4:14, 15, and 18 on these six lines. Leave a margin of at least ¾ inch (2 cm) on the right side.

*Write this sentence: **Avoid sin as you would avoid a skunk.***

Alignment	15	Letter Spacing	10
Slant	15	Neatness	20
Formation	15	Size	10
Word Spacing	5	Proportion	10
		Total	___

Lesson 19

Proper Margins

Aim of the Lesson

To teach the children not to crowd their words at the end of a line, but to maintain proper margins on both sides of the paper.

Comments to the Teacher

1. Discuss the paragraphs at the top of the page.

2. Draw a diagram of a paper on the blackboard, and demonstrate how children sometimes crowd words and letters in every available space. Point out how ugly it really looks.

3. Margins should be consistent as much as possible, so that a straight line could be drawn down each side. The distance from each edge should also be consistent for the two sides.

4. Remind your pupils that a word may be divided, between syllables, if there is not enough room for it on one line. Tell them to plan ahead as they approach the end of each line. Small adjustments in spacing can be made so that the right margin remains very nearly straight.

5. Make this lesson practical. Insist not only that the children keep good margins in penmanship, but also that they make it a habit to maintain good margins in all their daily work. You could occasionally draw lines on their papers to show them how they are doing.

Practice Sentences

1. Some people have skunks for pets.
2. The skunk is a useful animal.
3. Skunks eat insects, mice, frogs, and snakes.
4. Skunks can spray scent as far as 10 feet (3 meters).

Lesson 20 Review of Slant, Alignment, and Proportion

Grizzly bears should not be trusted too far. If they are wounded, or if they feel endangered, grizzly bears may attack and kill people. Grizzly bears weigh up to 1,000 pounds.

As you write this lesson, first think: How is the slant of my letters? Then think: How even are my letters across their tops and bottoms? Are they all the right height? Keep asking yourself these questions until you finish the lesson. And keep right on asking them as you write tomorrow's English paper.

Copy as much as you can of the paragraph about grizzly bears.

Alignment	15	Letter Spacing	10
Slant	15	Neatness	20
Formation	15	Size	10
Word Spacing	5	Proportion	5
		Total	___

41

Lesson 20

Review of Slant, Alignment, and Proportion

Aim of the Lesson

To review the practice of quality in the areas of slant, alignment, and proportion.

Comments to the Teacher

1. First of all, go over the instructions for the lesson. If the pupils finish the paragraph before they run out of space, they should begin again.

2. Next discuss the paragraph in the upper right corner of the page. Emphasize the need for children to go over and over these questions in their minds as they write. Be sure they understand what each of the terms means.

3. With a lesson of this nature, you can check on some things other than just the areas of quality that are drilled. You can check on writing speed, encouraging the slow ones to speed up as much as possible in the interest of efficiency, and the fast ones to slow down in the interest of accuracy and neatness. You can also check the evenness and smoothness of the writing and watch for good hand movement across the page.

4. In your grading, evaluate the last line only. Give priority to slant, alignment, and proportion.

Practice Sentences

1. The grizzly bear lives in the northern Rocky Mountains.
2. Grizzlies weight from 500 to 1,000 pounds (200 to 400 kg).
3. Silver-tip grizzlies have gray or white hairs.
4. Most grizzlies are black, dark gray, or brown.

Lesson 21 Capitals With Reverse Loops

Have you ever seen a cat 8 feet (2.5 meters) long? Yes, some cats are that big, but they are not house cats. One kind of big, wild cat that lives in the United States and Canada is called the cougar. The cougar has a frightening scream; but usually it is not dangerous and avoids people if it can.

We have already reviewed the capitals that start with loops made in the regular way. Today we will practice the two with reverse loops. They have the same size and slant that regular loops have, but the curve goes in the opposite direction.

Practice each letter in the spaces following.

C C

C C C

Also review the capitals that have regular loops.

F   *H*   *K*   *T*

M   *N*   *Q*   *W*

U   *V*   *Y*

X   *Z*

*Write these names: **Clifford, Carrie, Elaine, Elvin***

Alignment	15	Letter Spacing	10
Slant	15	Neatness	20
Formation	15	Size	10
Word Spacing	5	Proportion	5
		Total ____

43

Lesson 21

Capitals With Reverse Loops

Aim of the Lesson

To teach the children to form the letters *C* and *E* accurately and neatly.

Comments to the Teacher

1. After discussing the introductory paragraph, demonstrate the proper formation of a reverse loop beginning. Have the children practice it on the blackboard.

2. Cursive capital *C* and *E* are not the easiest letters to make well because they are so curving. But curving letters must still have good form, even though they have no straight lines. For example, in both of these letters, the junction of the two curves at the bottom of each letter should be very distinct and noticeable—like this: *C*, not like this: *C*. Also, the letter *E* should not have a stoop-shouldered appearance. It should be like a straight man leaning forward from his feet, not one who is bending at the waist.

3. The review of the loop capitals is important. Especially watch those loops to be sure they are made accurately and consistently.

Practice Sentences

1. Cougars sometimes kill deer to eat.
2. A cougar can hide so well that he is hard to see.
3. The cougar has a frightening cry.
4. The cougar likes to live in wild country.

Lesson 22   Capitals Beginning With Undercurves

The gopher is an underground animal. It spends most of its life a few inches to a foot (5 to 30 cm) below the ground. Though you may not often see a gopher, you can see the work that it does by the mounds of dirt that it piles up.

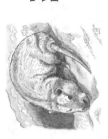

The six letters of this lesson all begin with undercurves, but that is about the only way in which they are all alike. You will need to learn how to make each one properly.

Copy each letter in the spaces following.

Write these names: ***Beverly, Gerald, Lydia, Paul, Royal, Sharon***

Alignment	15	Letter Spacing	10
Slant	15	Neatness	20
Formation	15	Size	10
Word Spacing	5	Proportion	10
		Total	___

Lesson 22

Capitals Beginning With Undercurves

Aim of the Lesson

To teach the children how to make the letters *B, G, L, P, R,* and *S* accurately and neatly.

Comments to the Teacher

1. The undercurve is not likely to need much practice, but you can give it a quick air drill if you so desire.

2. Read over the introductory paragraph at the top of the lesson.

3. Proceed to demonstrate and discuss each letter individually, taking note of the following points.

   a. The letter *B*: Try to keep the two "halves" about the same size; if anything, the bottom half should be the larger one.

   b. The Letter *G*: It should keep its shape. The second undercurve should sweep down halfway to the lowest alignment line, and the third undercurve should be kept *very* rounded.

   c. The letter *L*: It should be graceful, and the last double curve should go well below the base line.

   d. The letters *P* and *R*: The students should note their similarity.

   e. The letter *S*: The second part of the double curve should be *very* rounded; like *G*, this letter is difficult to keep in shape.

Practice Sentences

1. The gopher can do great harm to gardens.
2. Gophers eat the underground parts of vegetables.
3. Many larger animals like to eat gophers.
4. The gopher is about the size of a rat.

Lesson 23 Capitals Beginning With Overcurves, and Capital *D*

Few animals are much more lovely and graceful than the white-tailed deer. A deer is a swift animal that can cover 20 feet in a single leap when frightened. Deer are often hunted for their meat, which is called venison.

The capitals in this lesson are the "leftovers." The letters *A* and *O* are somewhat alike, and the letters *I* and *J* are somewhat alike. But the letter *D* is different from all the other capitals. Can you discover (before your teacher tells you) what makes *A* like *O* and *I* like *J*?

Practice each letter in the spaces following.

O O O

O O

I I I

J J

D D D

B A L P R A

Write these names: Arlene, Owen, Isaac, Janice, Donna

Alignment	15	Letter Spacing	10
Slant	15	Neatness	20
Formation	15	Size	10
Word Spacing	5	Proportion	10
		Total ___

47

Lesson 23

Capitals Beginning With Overcurves, and Capital *D*

Aim of the Lesson

To help the children learn to form the letters *A, O, I, J,* and *D* accurately and neatly.

Comments to the Teacher

1. Read over the introductory paragraph, and then stop and allow the children time to think. At least some of them should be able to see what makes the pairs of letters similar. The letters *A* and *O* both have ovals as the basis of their formation, and *I* and *J* both begin with the same type of overcurve that extends below the line.

2. Have the children air drill on the oval a few times.

3. You may need to put forth special effort to help the children form the letters *I* and *J* correctly. The first curve is often the key to good formation. Be sure that it starts below the line, and that it has a definite forward slant.

4. Be sure the back of the letter *J* stays straight.

5. The letter *D* is a more difficult one. The main problem is the *big* curve that gives the letter its roundness. It needs to touch the base line on its way around, and it should be very evenly curved.

Practice Sentences

1. Bucks shed their antlers each winter.
2. New antlers grow each summer.
3. White-tailed deer raise their white tails as a danger signal.
4. Mule deer live on the plains of western North America.

Lesson 24   Letter Spacing

The jaguar is a dangerous and ferocious cat with a loud, deep roar. The jaguar and the leopard look much the same, but they live a great distance apart. The jaguar lives in South and Central America and in Mexico.

Writing is hard to read if the letters are either crowded too close together or spread too far apart. But if our letters are all the same distance apart, and the right distance apart, our writing will be pleasant to read.

Write these words correctly in the line below them.

letters   too   close   too   far   apart   letters   just   right

Copy these sentences in the lines below them. Space your letters correctly.

You wouldn't want to get too close to an angry jaguar.

Don't let your letters get too close together either.

*Write this sentence: **Poorly spaced writing is hard to read.***

Alignment	15	Letter Spacing	10
Slant	15	Neatness	20
Formation	15	Size	10
Word Spacing	5	Proportion	10
		Total	___

Lesson 24

Letter Spacing

Aim of the Lesson

To teach the children to space their letters consistently, and to space them the right distance apart.

Comments to the Teacher

1. Discuss the introductory paragraph.

2. Look at the writing in the first line with the children. Discuss the appearance of all three kinds of spacing. Have the children decide personally which one is their writing. This will help them to decide what can be done about it.

3. Give the pupils some direction on how to maintain consistent and even spacing. One way to be sure of more even spacing is to avoid windshield-wiper style writing. When a writer must stretch his hand to reach the end of a word before he moves on to the next word, his writing is likely to be very crowded. On the other hand, if he moves down the line too fast, the letters will be spaced too far apart.

4. Supervise the children closely to be sure their spacing especially is correct.

Practice Sentences

1. Some South American jaguars weight more than 300 pounds (120 kg).
2. Jaguars live in the jungle.
3. The jaguar's voice sounds like coughing.
4. Jaguars delight to kill and eat cattle.

Lesson 25   Word Spacing

The leopard is much like the jaguar, but it lives in Africa and Asia. It is a large, spotted cat. The Bible mentions the leopard in Jeremiah 13:23: "Can the Ethiopian change his skin, or the leopard his spots?" A leopard can climb a tree carrying an animal as big as itself.

Good spacing between letters is important, and good spacing between words is just as important. The worst error in word spacing is writing the words too close together. Then the reader cannot tell where one word ends and the next begins. Too much space between words wastes paper, and it also makes reading unpleasant.

Copy these words, which finish the verse above.

"Then may ye also do good, that are accustomed to

do evil." Jeremiah 13:23

Copy this sentence.

It is hard to do right if we have been doing wrong.

Write this sentence: I want to do right always.

Alignment	15	Letter Spacing	10
Slant	15	Neatness	20
Formation	15	Size	10
Word Spacing	5	Proportion	10
		Total	___

Word Spacing

Aim of the Lesson

To help the children space their words the proper distance apart with consistent spacing between all their words.

Comments to the Teacher

1. Go over the introductory paragraph.

2. Demonstrate on the blackboard word spacing that is too close, too wide, and just right. Help the children to see that, especially when the words are written close together, the writing is sometimes very difficult to read. Perhaps you could run several short words together and see whether they can read them, such as "Isawacat." That will help them to get the point.

3. The children should be told that the general rule for word spacing is to leave enough space so that one medium-sized letter, like *a*, could be written between the words. If this rule is followed, the writing will be quite legible.

4. As a rule, writing is the most legible all around when the words are fairly compact and there is good spacing between them.

Practice Sentences

1. Leopards can climb trees as easily as monkeys.
2. Most leopards are yellow with black spots.
3. Some leopards are 8 feet (2½ meters) long.
4. Some leopards like the ice and snow of high mountains.

Lesson 26 Some Difficult Small Letters

Killer whales can be quite vicious, sometimes attacking and eating dolphins and other sea creatures. But usually their behavior is better than their name sounds. Killer whales travel in groups and are found in all the oceans.

In our writing, we all find that some letters are easier to make than others. Each person finds different letters that are hard for him to make. But there are some letters that *most* people find difficult. This lesson and the next two lessons contain some of these.

Practice these difficult letters until you can make them right. Copy each one at least ten times.

k

r

s

*Write these words on the line below: **baker, river, busy, pack, barely, sun***

Alignment	15	Letter Spacing	10	
Slant	15	Neatness	20	
Formation	15	Size	10	
Word Spacing	5	Proportion	10	
		Total		

Lesson 26

Some Difficult Small Letters

Aim of the Lesson

To help the children with formation of some of the more difficult lower-case letters.

Comments to the Teacher

1. The children may not think there is anything wrong with the way they make these letters. Perhaps there is not, but more likely there is. So do not take the children's word for it. Check each letter.

2. The letter *k* is frequently made incorrectly in these ways: closing the loop in the middle of the letter (*k*) and changing the final slant-undercurve into just one big undercurve. These two often go together.

3. The letter *r* is frequently made incorrectly in these ways: making just a rounded hump (*∩*), making a point (*∧*), or making the top square (*∏*). Again emphasize the strokes used to form this letter correctly.

4. The letter *s* is frequently given a very poor form and shape. It may be made too flat (*◢*), to straight (*△*), or distorted in many ways. Be sure it is made gracefully according to correct form.

5. The letter *c* often does not have good form. To achieve that, it needs a noticeable (though rounded) point at the bottom before the final undercurve. It should also have a definite hook on the top to keep it from being mistaken for an *i*.

Practice Sentences

1. Killer whales do not eat people.
2. The killer whale is a very smart animal.
3. A more honorable name for the killer whale is orca whale.
4. Is my behavior always what it should be?

Lesson 27   More Difficult
               Small Letters

God has made hundreds of kinds of mice. The house mouse is probably the most familiar one. In the winter it likes to come indoors where it can be warm. Mice eat almost anything people eat, but they damage much more than they eat. The house mouse is found almost all over the world.

Mice are very hard to catch. We set traps and put out poison, but still they are hard to get rid of. Sometimes it is also hard to catch all the small mistakes that keep our writing from looking neat. Let us try hard to form correctly the four letters in this lesson.

Practice these difficult letters until you can make them right. Copy each one at least ten times.

b

e

r

x

*Write this sentence: **Does my letter e have a straight back?***

Alignment	15	Letter Spacing	10
Slant	15	Neatness	20
Formation	15	Size	10
Word Spacing	5	Proportion	10
		Total	___

More Difficult Small Letters

Aim of the Lesson

To help the children with formation of some of the more difficult lower-case letters.

Comments to the Teacher

1. The letter *b* may have a tendency to lose its straight back. Help the children to keep this letter from bending. Two other common problems are the second undercurve nearly touching the slant line (*ƀ*) or else being too far away (*ℓ*).

2. It is difficult to make the letter *e* with the two qualities that it needs to be a letter with good form. It should have both a straight back and an open loop.

3. Be sure that the second stroke of *x* actually slants forward. The difference between the second stroke and the line that crosses it is the difference between a cursive slant stroke and a manuscript forward-slanting line.

4. The children's *z*'s need to appear straight, even though there is hardly a straight line in this letter. The hook should be small and neat.

Practice Sentences

1. Mice eat almost anything people eat.
2. Mice have from 30 to 60 baby mice each year.
3. The jumping mouse can jump 10 to 12 feet (3 to 4 meters) in one hop!
4. The color of most mice is brown or gray.

Lesson 28   Difficult Capital Letters

The best known rat in the United States is the brown rat. Years ago this rat lived only in Asia. It found its way to America on ships. Rats carry diseases, and they destroy many dollars' worth of grain and food every year.

Like rats, difficult letters can cause much trouble, and the hardest of them all are the capitals. This lesson drills some of the hardest capitals.

Practice these difficult capital letters in the spaces following them.

$\mathscr{F}$

$\mathscr{H}$

$\mathscr{A}$

$\mathscr{I}$

$\mathscr{D}$

$\mathscr{Z}$

Alignment	15	Letter Spacing	20
Slant	15	Neatness	10
Formation	15	Size	10
Word Spacing	5	Proportion	10
		Total	___

Write these words: **Fox, Goat, Sheep, Ibis, Dog, Zebra**

Lesson 28

Difficult Capital Letters

Aim of the Lesson

To help the children with the formation of difficult capitals, and to give them practice in writing them.

Comments to the Teacher

1. Almost all the capitals are more difficult to form than the small letters. But the six capitals in this lesson can be really difficult. If you know of other capitals that your pupils need special practice on, this would be the time to work on those as well. The children will probably be quite willing to tell you which letters are hard for them.

2. The thing that makes these letters difficult is the lack of straight lines. The only straight line in them all is the short slant of the letter *F*. Therefore, the main problem your children will have is maintaining accurate and consistent form. If they do make the letter *I* correctly one time, for example, it might be difficult for them to get it correct the next time. The key is practice, practice, and more practice.

3. Here are some things to watch in these letters:
   a. The formation of the loop-curve of the letter *F*.
   b. The second and the third curve of the letter *G*.
   c. The double curve of the letter *S*.
   d. The correct overall form of the letter *I*.
   e. The large double curve of the letter *D*.
   f. The general straightness and good form of the letter *Z*.

Practice Sentences

1. The rat is found all over the world.
2. The pack rat carries off bright objects.
3. Many animals like to kill and eat rats.
4. Rats are much large than mice.

Lesson 29   Quality Checkup

Do you remember the names of the different areas of writing quality? What do they mean?

Slant. Letters should be slanted forward and all slanted the same.

Alignment. Letters should be even across the tops and bottoms.

Height and Proportion. Each letter should be the right height with each part in correct proportion.

Size. Letters should be neither too large nor too small.

Spacing. All letters and words should be spaced a proper distance apart.

Formation. Each letter should be formed properly.

Copy the verse below.

" The fear of man bringeth a snare: but whoso putteth

his trust in the Lord shall be safe." Proverbs 29:25

Write this sentence: **My writing must be correct and neat.**

Alignment	15	Letter Spacing 10
Slant	15	Neatness 20
Formation	15	Size 10
Word Spacing	5	Proportion 10
		Total ___

59

Lesson 29

Quality Checkup

Aim of the Lesson

To review the various areas of writing quality and to be sure that each student is striving for top quality writing in his everyday schoolwork.

Comments to the Teacher

1. Discuss the seven areas of quality with the children. Be sure they understand the meaning of each. Demonstrate wherever the children may have forgotten terms and their meanings.

2. This is a final quality review before the test. As the children copy the verse, give final reminders on the areas in which each child is lacking. Remind them of the test, and urge them to improve now so that the test will show a good grade. (Of course, the motivation should be deeper than that too.)

3. Encourage the children to write the last sentence as perfectly as they possibly can. It should show that they have improved in their handwriting during the past year.

Practice Sentences

Use the sentences after "Slant," "Alignment," and so forth (on the pupil's page). If any more practice sentences are needed, Bible memory work may be used.

Lesson 30   Final Test

This is your final test in penmanship for Grade 4. How much have you improved during the past year?

In this test, write the sentence in the upper right corner of this page. When you have completed that, write in cursive all the capital letters of the alphabet.

Write this sentence:

God wants us to be fair, just, kind, loving, and happy; zealous and exact in all our work; and quiet at the right times.

Formation	52	Size and
Alignment	10	Proportion	10
Slant	10	Speed	8
Spacing	10	Total ____

Lesson 30

Final Test

Directions to the Teacher

1. Ask the children whether they have any questions about any area of quality or the formation of any letter. Explain any difficulties before the test so that the children (as well as you) are satisfied that they are prepared.

2. Explain the basis on which the test will be evaluated. The children should be careful to make every capital and small letter accurately, to practice every area of quality, and to finish the test in a reasonable amount of time.

3. Discuss the material at the top of the lesson, and be sure the children understand the directions. Then have them proceed with the test. Be sure you do not give them any help except directional help during the test. Do not let them go beyond about twenty minutes for the test.

4. On the evaluation chart, the fifty-two points for formation include one point for each small and each capital letter. Deduct for "Speed" if it is obvious that the writing was done too slowly or too quickly.

5. Let the children know which areas of quality they are weak in and which letters they have formed incorrectly, so that they can improve in those areas.